RESILIENT MINDS

A JOURNEY FROM SHADOWS TO LIGHT

SAPTAPARNA CHANDRA

ISBN 979-8-89556-043-3

Dedication

To Mrs. Bipasha Mukherjee, whose guidance illuminated my path and whose unwavering support helped me through my challenging times.

To my husband Mr Indrajit Chandra, for his constant encouragement, and to my children Aaditya and Aparajita, for their boundless love and patience—thank you for being my constant source of strength.

– Saptaparna Chandra

Contents

About the Author

Saptaparna Chandra is an accomplished professional with a rich educational background, holding a B. Tech in Electronics and Telecommunication and a Post Graduate Diploma in Business Administration from the esteemed Vinod Gupta School of Management (VGSOM) at IIT Kharagpur. A proud alumna of South Point High School, she has built an impressive career spanning 14 years in the corporate sector, contributing her expertise to renowned companies such as L&T, Tata Communications Limited, and Vodafone.

Currently, Saptaparna serves as the Assistant Head of the MBA Department at the Institute of Engineering and Management in Kolkata. Her extensive experience in the corporate world, coupled with her role as an educator, has provided her with deep insights into the challenges faced by the younger generation. Through her interactions with teenagers and young adults, she has observed a growing prevalence of neuro-divergent issues, affecting not only the individuals themselves but also their caregivers, stakeholders, and surrounding communities.

Driven by a desire to shed light on these challenges, Saptaparna has authored a collection of

12 short stories, each offering a unique perspective on the complexities of neuro-divergence. Her stories are a compassionate exploration of the struggles faced by those navigating these issues, offering a message of hope and resilience. Through her writing, Saptaparna aims to remind readers that they are not alone in their battles and that, despite the darkness, there is always a light at the end of the tunnel. Her work is a heartfelt invitation to pause, appreciate the beauty of life, and find solace in the shared human experience.

Finding His Way: A Story of Hope and Acceptance

Aryan had always found school difficult. Words and numbers seemed to dance on the page, twisting and turning in ways that didn't make sense to him. While other kids could read a paragraph in seconds, it took Aryan minutes—painful, frustrating minutes that left him feeling foolish and defeated. He wasn't lazy or careless, but no matter how hard he tried, the letters wouldn't stay in place, and the numbers never added up the way they should.

His teachers at school were kind, but they didn't understand. They told him to try harder. *"Please pay more attention, Aryan!"* said his teachers. But Aryan was already giving everything he had. The harder he tried, the worse he felt. His grades slipped, and he began to dread going to school, knowing that another day of failure awaited him.

The other kids didn't make it any easier. They teased him for stumbling over his words, for getting confused in math, for being different. Aryan wanted to fit in, to be like everyone else. But no matter how much he wished for it, he couldn't change the way his brain worked. His friends, once close, started to drift away. They didn't understand why Aryan couldn't keep up, and eventually, they stopped inviting him to hang out after school, to birthday parties, to any social gatherings. In class when students distributed sweets on their birthdays, he always got one, whereas others were graced with two. It seemed to Aryan as if he was being punished for something, which he had no clue.

One day, after yet another failed test, the school called Aryan's parents in for a meeting. The Principal, looking uncomfortable, gently suggested that Aryan might do better in a school that could cater to his needs—a school for special children.

Aryan sat outside the office, his heart pounding, as his parents discussed the possibility with the Principal. He didn't want to leave his school, even though it was hard. It was his school, with his friends, and he didn't want to be sent away like there was something wrong with him. But when his parents came out of the meeting, their faces solemn, Aryan knew things were going to change.

The new school was different from the moment Aryan walked through the doors. He was walking through the corridor holding his father's hand tightly. His throat was chocked and he felt like crying. The new school was smaller, quieter than his earlier school. The classrooms were filled with kids who seemed a lot like him—kids who struggled with reading, writing, and Maths, just like he did. The teachers smiled warmly and introduced themselves one by one, but Aryan couldn't shake off the feeling of being an outsider.

His parents had tried to explain that this new school was designed to help him. The teachers who are called Special Educators, understood how to teach kids like him, but Aryan didn't want to be there. He missed his old school, his old friends, and the familiar routines he had known for so long. Every morning, he woke up hoping it was all just a bad dream and he would get to go back to his old life.

But the days passed, and Aryan had to face the reality that this was his new normal. His parents kept reassuring him that they had made this decision to help him. They wanted him to succeed and be happy, but all Aryan felt was lost. He couldn't understand why he had to leave everything behind? Why he had to be the one who was different? All his old friends could study in his earlier school, then why will he not be allowed?

Aryan's new teachers were patient and kind to him and they always tried to help him. But at first, he resisted their efforts and shunned their assistance. He kept his head down, avoiding eye contact, and did the bare minimum in class. When they asked him to read aloud or solve a problem on the board, he would shake his head. His cheeks flushed with embarrassment. He remembered those staring eyes from his earlier school. He remembered his friend's giggles whenever he went up to the board. Whenever he closed his eyes, he could visualize them. He didn't want to be singled out again like before. He didn't want to draw attention to his struggles.

But the best part here is that his teachers didn't give up on him. They noticed how Aryan struggled, how he held himself back. They knew that he needed time. They approached him gently, offering support without pressure. They made sure that Aryan knew he was safe in their classroom, that no one was judging him. They were very patient with him and was ready to wait till he was ready to trust them. They focused on building his faith first and bond with him.

One day, during a reading lesson, Mrs. Khan, one of his teachers, sat down beside him. "Aryan," she said softly, "*I know reading is hard for you, but that doesn't mean you can't do it. We're going to take it one step at a time, okay? You don't have to rush. Just do your best.*"

For the first time in a long while, Aryan looked up. There was no frustration in Mrs. Khan's eyes, no impatience. Just understanding. He nodded hesitantly, and she handed him a book that was easier than the ones he had struggled with before.

He slowly made his way through the first page, sounding out each word with Mrs. Khan's help. As he went through the first page something clicked. He realised that it wasn't easy. But for the first time, Aryan felt like he was making progress. The words didn't seem as daunting, the sentences were not as impossible. Mrs. Khan's encouragement gave him the confidence to keep going.

Over the next few weeks, Aryan began to open up more. His teachers continued to support him, breaking down lessons into manageable parts, and celebrating each small victory. They taught him new strategies to deal with his difficulties. They helped him with tools and techniques that made reading and writing a little easier.

Aryan began to realize that he wasn't dumb; he just learned differently. The new school wasn't a punishment—it was a place where he could finally understand things at his own pace. His teachers weren't there to judge him, but to help him succeed. The shame and embarrassment that had weighed him down started to lift. He felt so light, as if a burden has been taken away from him.

Aryan also started to make new friends. The other kids at the school understood what it was like to struggle, and they didn't judge him for it. He found himself laughing again, joining in on conversations, and even helping others who were having a tough time. The school that once felt so foreign was becoming a place where Aryan felt he belonged.

By the end of the school year, Aryan was a different person. He was no longer the boy who felt like a failure, who dreaded school and shied away from challenges. He had found his confidence, thanks to the teachers who never gave up on him and the friends who accepted him for who he was.

Aryan's parents were overjoyed at the change in their son. They saw the light in his eyes, the pride he took in his work, and they knew they had made the right decision, even though it had been a difficult one.

One afternoon, Aryan came home with a smile on his face, holding a book he had read all by himself. He couldn't wait to show his parents, to prove that he was capable, that he could do it. *"Mom, Dad, Look!"* he said, holding up the book. *"I read the whole book!"* His parents hugged him, their eyes filled with tears of joy. *"We're so proud of you, Aryan,"* his mother said. *"You've worked so hard, and look how far you've come."* Aryan beamed with pride. He had found his place, his confidence, and a new sense of hope for the future.

Aryan never forgot his old school or the friends he had left behind, but he no longer wished to go back. He had found something even more valuable—a place where he could learn, grow, and thrive, surrounded by people who believed in him.

The journey hadn't been easy, but Aryan had found his way. He had learned that being different wasn't something to be ashamed of, and that with the right support, he could achieve anything. As he looked forward to the next school year, Aryan felt ready to take on any challenge. He knew that he was stronger and more capable than he had ever imagined.

The story touches on the struggles of living with Dyslexia, especially in an environment that doesn't always understand or accommodate those challenges. It also highlights the importance of support from parents, teachers and other associated institutions which should never give up on the child.

The Unseen Struggles

Rohan sat at his desk, staring at the Maths book in front of him. Numbers swam across the page, blurring together until they became an indecipherable mess. His fingers drummed nervously on the desk, a habit that had earned him more than a few stern looks from his teachers. Today was no different. Mrs. Sharma's voice broke through his thoughts, sharp and impatient. *"Rohan! Pay attention! We're on question seven."* He nodded quickly, pretending to follow along, but his mind was already elsewhere, wandering through a labyrinth of distractions. The hum of the ceiling fan, the rustle of papers, and the faint sound of footsteps in the hallway—all of it competed for his attention, pulling him away from the task at hand. *"Focus,"* he whispered to himself, trying to force the numbers back into place. But the harder he tried, the more elusive they became. It seemed like all the surrounding noises made it impossible for him to focus on his work. He looked around the class and found all his classmates doing their work with full attention and concentration. He felt bad with his inability. He felt as if he is not a part of this class and he was not supposed to belong here.

School had always been a struggle for Rohan. Diagnosed with ADHD at a young age of 6 years. As soon as his diagnosis was done, his parents left no stone unturned to bring in all possible interventions to help him cope with this. He had spent countless hours in different types of therapies. Sensory sessions to help him manage the overwhelming input from the world around him. He had issues with the sensation created by different fabrics of his clothes. Some clothes made him feel calm, whereas some of them made him feel irritable. It started improving after the regular therapies. One more type of therapy was also very helpful. Occupational therapy, it helped to develop the skills he needed to function in a classroom. But despite all the support, the world still felt too loud, too bright, too chaotic for him to handle.

His parents, Sunil and Priya, were his biggest advocates. Initially they were unable to understand what wrong they did which caused this. They were getting in the fault-finding mode. It was all blaming each other and asking the question repeatedly to themselves *'Why us?'* They were also undergoing parental counselling classes which helped them to cope as a caregiver. During one of their classes, the Counsellor Dr Ganguly explained to them that *'Imagine your son is unable to see properly. How will you cope with this?'* Priya replied, '*We will take him to an Ophthalmologist. We will get his eyes checked and get him spectacles if suggested.'*

Dr Ganguly said *"Excellent! So you will give him some tool to cope with his sight issue. You have to do the same thing here as well. These therapies are going to help him cope with his difficulties. Once he learns to handle them, you can't imagine how well he improvises and makes it easier for him.'*

Hearing this was music to their eyes. They could see a ray of light at the end of the tunnel. Till now it was only darkness, such suffocating darkness. They decided to fight till the end. They fought tirelessly to get him the help he needed, attending every meeting, reading every article, and following every piece of advice the doctors gave. At home, they created a structured environment. They broke every task into small jobs which was more manageable for Rohan, using visual schedules. They celebrated even the smallest victories in a grand way. Seeing the smile on Rohan's face gave them much satisfaction.

But no matter what they did, Rohan's struggles persisted. Homework took hours, his grades were slipping, and his teachers often called Priya or sent notes in the school diary to express their concerns. The more the school year progressed, the more Rohan felt like he was drowning in expectations he couldn't meet.

At night, when he was supposed to be sleeping, Rohan would often hear his parents talking in hushed tones.

"I'm worried about him, Sunil" Priya would say. *"What will he do when we're not around? How will he manage on his own?"*

Sunil's voice would come, gentle but strained. *"We'll figure it out, Priya. He's smart, he's kind, and we'll keep supporting him. We have to believe he'll find his way."*

Rohan knew they loved him, but their worry seeped into his own thoughts. What if they were right? What if he never learned how to cope? What if he couldn't survive in a world that demanded so much focus, so much attention to detail?

One day, after a particularly rough morning at school, Rohan found himself wandering into the small garden behind his house. It was his sanctuary, a secret place where he could be alone with his thoughts, away from the pressures of school and therapy sessions. He sat down on the swing, gently swaying back and forth, trying to calm the storm inside his head.

He thought about his parents, about their worry and their unwavering support. He thought about the teachers who always seemed disappointed in him, and the classmates who never understood why he couldn't just *"try harder."* Most of all, he thought about himself—the boy who was always struggling to fit into a world that felt too big, too overwhelming.

As he sat there, a small butterfly fluttered past, its wings a blur of orange and black. Rohan watched it, fascinated by its erratic flight. The butterfly didn't move in a straight line, nor did it follow any predictable pattern. It zigzagged, looped, and hovered, seemingly without direction. But it was beautiful in its own way, navigating the world on its own terms.

For the first time in a long while, Rohan felt a glimmer of hope. Maybe he didn't have to follow the same path as everyone else. Maybe, like the butterfly, he could find his own way to navigate the world—a way that embraced his differences rather than trying to force him into a pre-set mould he couldn't fit.

The thought was comforting, and he held onto it as he went back inside, ready to face the challenges that awaited him. His parents were there, as they always were, with encouraging smiles and open arms. They didn't have all the answers, but they had each other, and for now, that was enough.

Rohan knew the road ahead wouldn't be easy, and the future still loomed uncertain. But as long as he had his family by his side, he believed he could keep trying, keep searching for his own way through the chaos. And maybe, just maybe, that would be enough to carry him through.

***

The story touches on the struggles of living with ADHD, especially in an environment that doesn't always understand or accommodate those challenges. It also highlights the importance of support and the hope that comes from finding one's own path in life.

***

The Alchemy of Resilience

The pharmaceutical business was resonant with the name Maya Verma. Distinguished by her keen intellect, inventive concepts, and unwavering determination, she had constructed a prosperous commercial enterprise from its foundation. Verma Pharmaceuticals, her company, was a pioneer in innovative medical research and development. Her impact was felt well outside of the labs and boardrooms. Maya was seen by the world as a symbol of achievement since she had surmounted every challenge to rise to the position of one of the most influential people in the sector. But behind the polished facade of success lay a story of pain, struggle, and resilience that few knew.

Maya's journey had not been an easy one. As a child, she was often labelled "difficult" by teachers and peers. She had severe behavioural issues, struggling with anger, defiance, and a constant need to challenge authority. Her parents, unsure of how to handle her, sought help from various doctors and psychologists, but the interventions offered little relief. Maya's strong-willed nature often clashed with those around her, and she grew up feeling misunderstood and isolated.

Despite these challenges, Maya excelled academically. She channelled her inner turmoil into her studies, finding solace in the world of science. She was fascinated by chemistry and biology, captivated by the idea of using science to heal and transform. It was this passion that led her to pursue a degree in pharmaceutical sciences, and later, to establish her own company. But even as she achieved success in her professional life, Maya's personal life remained fraught with difficulties.

Maya's marriage was a dark chapter in her life. She had married Arjun, a charming and ambitious man, believing that they shared the same values and dreams. But the reality of their relationship soon became a nightmare. Arjun was physically and verbally abusive, his cruelty hidden behind a mask of charisma that fooled everyone else. He belittled Maya's accomplishments, sought to control her every move, and used violence to assert his dominance.

For years, Maya endured the abuse in silence. She was trapped by societal expectations, by the fear of judgment, and by the hope that things might one day get better. But when she discovered she was pregnant, something inside her snapped. The thought of raising a child in such a toxic environment was unbearable. She knew she had to leave, to protect herself and her unborn child, no matter the cost.

One night, after a particularly brutal altercation, Maya made the decision to walk away. With nothing but a suitcase and her unborn child, she left Arjun and never looked back. It was one of the hardest decisions she had ever made, but it was also the most liberating one. For the first time in years, she felt a sense of control over her life, a sense of hope for the future.

Raising her daughter, Aisha, as a single mother was challenging, but Maya was determined to give her the love and stability she had never known. She poured all her energy into her work and her child, building her company from a small startup to a Global powerhouse. But as Aisha grew older, Maya began to notice troubling signs.

Aisha was not like other children. She was defiant, prone to explosive tantrums, and constantly testing boundaries. Her behaviour was erratic and unpredictable, swinging between intense affection and uncontrollable anger. Maya, who had faced her own behavioural challenges as a child, recognized the signs but was unprepared for the severity of Aisha's condition.

When Aisha was eight years old, Maya took her to a specialist who diagnosed her with Oppositional Defiant Disorder (ODD). The diagnosis was a blow to Maya. She had hoped that by providing Aisha with a loving and stable environment, she could protect her from the struggles she had faced. But the reality was far more complicated.

Aisha's ODD made every day a battle. She resisted authority, argued incessantly, and often lashed out in anger. School was a nightmare, with teachers constantly calling to report her disruptive behaviour. Maya, who had built her career on solving complex problems, felt helpless in the face of her daughter's struggles. She tried everything—therapy, behaviour modification programs, even alternative treatments—but nothing seemed to work.

The stress took a toll on Maya. Running a successful business while caring for a child with severe behavioural issues left her exhausted and emotionally drained. She questioned herself constantly, wondering if she was failing as a mother, if she had made the right decisions, if she could ever find a way to help Aisha.

But Maya was not one to give up. She had faced down her own demons and survived earlier, and she was determined to do the same for her daughter. Slowly, she began to shift her approach. Instead of focusing solely on trying to *"fix"* Aisha's behaviour, she started to understand her daughter's perspective. She learned to pick her battles, to set clear but reasonable expectations, and to provide Aisha with consistent love and support, even when it seemed like nothing was working.

Maya also sought out a support network, connecting with other parents who had children with similar challenges. These connections served as a vital lifeline, offering her advice, empathy, and the reassurance that she was not alone in her struggles. She learned to advocate fiercely for her daughter, ensuring that Aisha received the accommodations she needed at school and in therapy.

As the years passed, there were no miracles, but there were small victories. Aisha continued to struggle with ODD, but she also began to develop her own strengths. She had a sharp mind, a quick wit, and a fierce sense of justice. Maya encouraged these traits, guiding her daughter to channel her defiance into positive outlets, like debate and advocacy. Aisha participated in debate competitions in school and did remarkably well. Over time, she learned to manage her emotions better, and while the challenges never fully went away, they became more manageable.

Through it all, Maya's love for her daughter never wavered. She had learned the hard way that there were no easy answers, no quick fixes. But she had also learned the power of resilience, of facing challenges head-on and refusing to let them define you. She taught Aisha to embrace her own strength, to understand that her struggles did not make her less valuable, but rather, more human.

In the end, Maya's greatest success was not her business empire, but the relationship she built with her daughter. She had learned to see beyond the diagnosis, beyond the behavioural issues, to the person Aisha truly was—a strong, intelligent, and compassionate young woman who, like her mother, would one day change the world in her own way.

Maya Verma's story was not just one of professional success, but of personal triumph—of overcoming abuse, of raising a child with severe challenges, and of finding the strength to love and support that child unconditionally. It was a story of resilience, of the alchemy that turns pain into power, and of the enduring bond between a mother and her daughter.

⋘❁❁❁⋙

This story highlights the journey of a mother who overcame personal trauma and the challenges of raising a child with a severe behavioural disorder, emphasizing the themes of resilience, unconditional love, and the power of understanding and support in the face of adversity.

⋘❁❁❁⋙

Story 4#

The Equation of Love

Dr. Anil Mehta was a man who had spent his life solving the most complex mathematical problems. Renowned worldwide for his contributions to the field, his mind was a fortress of logic and precision. Equations were his language, and numbers were his friends. He had won numerous awards, given lectures at prestigious universities, and was revered by his peers. But despite all his achievements, nothing gave him more pride than his family—especially his daughter, Riya.

Riya was the apple of Anil's eye. From the moment she was born, he imagined her following in his footsteps, excelling in academics, and perhaps even surpassing his own accomplishments. He often daydreamed about teaching her advanced mathematics, the two of them bonding over complex problems, and her eventually becoming a mathematical prodigy.

But reality, as Anil was soon to learn, doesn't always follow the neat, logical patterns of mathematics.

When Riya turned five, her school called Anil and his wife, Nandini, for a meeting. Anil walked into the principal's office, confident and assured, expecting to hear glowing reports about his daughter. Instead, he was met with concern.

"Mr and Mrs Mehta," the teacher began hesitantly, *"We've noticed that Riya is struggling with reading and writing. She's falling behind her classmates, and we believe it would be beneficial for her to undergo a psychometric test. It might help us understand if there are any learning difficulties that need to be addressed."*

Anil's heart froze. The teacher's words echoed in his mind, clashing with everything he believed about his daughter. How could Riya—his daughter—be struggling with something as basic as reading and writing? The very suggestion that she might have a learning difficulty felt like an insult to his intelligence, to his legacy.

He clenched his fists, his anger bubbling just beneath the surface. *"Are you suggesting that my daughter is… what, slow? Incompetent?"* he snapped, glaring at the teacher.

"Mr Mehta, that's not what we're saying," the teacher replied calmly. *"We just want to understand how we can better support Riya's learning. Sometimes, children need a different approach, and this test could help us identify that."*

Anil wasn't listening. His mind was already racing, searching for explanations. He couldn't accept that his daughter—his brilliant daughter—could have any sort of problem. The fault had to lie elsewhere.

"This is ridiculous," Anil declared, his voice rising. *"If Riya is struggling, it's because this school is not doing its job properly. You're not challenging her enough, or you're not teaching her correctly. I refuse to believe that there's anything wrong with my daughter."*

The teacher tried to interject, but Anil was beyond reasoning. He stood up abruptly, pulling Nandini up with him. *"We're leaving. Riya will not be subjected to any ridiculous tests. I'll find her a better school, one that knows how to educate a child properly."*

As they stormed out of the school, Nandini's heart was heavy. She had seen Riya's struggles at home—the way her daughter avoided reading, how she would get frustrated when trying to write, the tears that would well up in her eyes when she couldn't keep up with her classmates. But Anil's anger left no room for her concerns. He was adamant that the school was at fault, and Nandini, feeling helpless, didn't dare contradict him.

That evening, Anil's anger hadn't subsided. He paced around their living room, venting his frustration. *"How could this happen, Nandini? We've given Riya everything she needs. How could she be struggling like this? And you… you're at home with her all day. What have you been doing? Isn't it your job to make sure she's learning?"*

Nandini flinched at his words, her eyes welling up with tears. *"Anil, I'm doing my best. I've tried to help her, but… I don't know how to make it easier for her. I see her struggling, and it breaks my heart. I just want her to be happy."*

Anil's harsh words hung in the air, their weight pressing down on both of them. Nandini retreated into silence, her pain evident, but Anil was too consumed by his own emotions to notice. He was a man who used to finding solutions, but this—this was a problem he didn't know how to solve.

True to his word, Anil found a new school for Riya. But the change didn't bring the results he had hoped for. Riya continued to struggle, her difficulties only becoming more pronounced. The teachers at the new school were kind, but they too suggested that Riya might have a learning difficulty. Each time, Anil dismissed their concerns, insisting that Riya just needed more time, more discipline, more of anything except what they were suggesting.

But deep down, as the months passed, a seed of doubt began to grow in Anil's mind. He couldn't deny the evidence before him—Riya was not thriving, and his anger wasn't helping her. Every day, he saw the frustration and sadness in her eyes, and it tore him apart. How could a man who had spent his life solving the most complex equations be so utterly unable to help his own daughter?

One night, after a particularly difficult day with Riya, Nandini approached Anil in the quiet of their bedroom. Her voice was soft, but there was a resolve in her eyes that Anil hadn't seen before.

"Anil," she began, *"we need to face the reality of what's happening. Riya is struggling, and it's not because of the school or because of anything we've done wrong. She needs help, real help, and we can't keep denying that."*

Anil looked at her, the defensiveness rising within him once more. But before he could not speak, Nandini continued. *"I know this is hard for you to accept,"* she said, *"but this isn't about you, or me, or your legacy. This is about Riya, and what she needs from us. She needs us to be her parents, not her teachers, not her critics. We need to listen to her, to the experts, and to each other. Blaming won't help her. Only love and support will"*.

Anil felt a lump form in his throat, the walls he had built around his heart began to crack. He looked at Nandini. Seeing the pain and the strength in her eyes, he realized how much he had hurt her with his words, how much he had failed to see her own struggles and fears

For the first time, Anil allowed himself to truly listen, to let go of his pride and accept that he didn't have all the answers. He wrapped his arms around Nandini, holding her tightly, and whispered, *"I'm sorry. I'm so sorry. I've been so focused on what I wanted Riya to be that I didn't see what she needed. I've been a fool."*

Nandini held him back, tears streaming down her face. *"We'll get through this together, Anil. We'll find the right help for Riya, and we'll give her all the love and support she needs. That's all that matters."*

The next day, Anil and Nandini made the decision to consult with specialists. They found a psychologist who conducted the psychometric tests and diagnosed Riya with Dyslexia. It was a difficult truth to accept, but it also came with a sense of relief. Now they knew what they were dealing with, and they could begin to help their daughter in the ways she needed.

Anil immersed himself in learning about Dyslexia, applying his analytical mind to understand the challenges Riya faced. But more importantly, he began to focus on what truly mattered—being a father who loved and supported his daughter, not just a mathematician expecting perfection.

With the right support, Riya began to make progress. She still struggled with reading and writing, but she also began to find her own strengths. She was creative, imaginative, and had a remarkable memory for stories. Anil learned to celebrate these strengths, to encourage her in ways that made her feel valued and understood.

In the end, Anil discovered that the most important equation he could ever solve was the one that balanced love, patience, and understanding. And in that equation, he found a new kind of fulfilment, one that no professional achievement could ever match.

This story highlights the journey of a father coming to terms with his daughter's learning difficulties, and the importance of letting go of expectations to embrace and support the child for who they are. It also touches on the impact of pride, the importance of humility, and the power of love and understanding within a family.

Story 5#

The Melody of Mitushi

Mitushi was different. Even as a baby, her parents, Leela and Parth, had noticed the little things—the way she didn't respond to her name, how she avoided their gaze, how she never babbled or cooed like other infants. By the time Mitushi was one year old, the doctors had confirmed what her parents had already begun to suspect: Mitushi was on the Autism spectrum.

As she grew, Mitushi's world was a place of patterns and predictability. She found comfort in routines—the way her mother braided her hair each morning, the exact placement of her toys on the shelf, the rhythm of her father's voice as he read her favourite story each night. Any disruption to these routines would throw her into a state of panic. She would cry, scream, and flail her arms, her small body overwhelmed by the chaos of a world she couldn't control.

Play school was a bewildering place for Mitushi. The other children were loud and lively, always running around, shouting, and playing games that seemed strange and confusing to her. Mitushi preferred to sit quietly, stacking blocks in precise rows, or lining up toy cars by colour. She rarely spoke, and when she did, it was often just to repeat what someone else had said, a habit called echolalia that she couldn't seem to stop.

The other kids didn't understand her. They would giggle and make fun of her when she repeated their words back to them like a parrot. Sometimes they would try to break her carefully arranged lines of toys just to see her reaction. Mitushi would become distraught. Her world spiralling out of control as she tried desperately to fix what had been disrupted. But the more she tried, the more they laughed, and the more isolated she felt.

Her teachers tried their level best to help her, but they were often at a loss. Mitushi's inability to communicate made it hard to reach her. Also her violent outbursts when things didn't go according to her internal script, made the other children wary of playing with her. She spent most of her days in a corner, quietly observing the world around her, never fully a part of it.

Leela and Parth were heartbroken to see their daughter struggling so much. They had enrolled her in speech therapy, hoping it would help her find her voice. The therapist, Mrs. Iyer, was kind and patient. She worked with Mitushi to slowly coax words from her. It was a slow process, filled with many setbacks. But over time, Mitushi began to speak, haltingly at first, but with growing confidence.

Even with these small victories, Mitushi's world remained difficult. The sensory overload of play school, the unpredictable behaviour of her peers, and the constant pressure to fit in, left her feeling overwhelmed and misunderstood. She would often come home in tears, her tiny hands clenched into fists, her body rigid with frustration.

One day, after a particularly tough day at school, Leela noticed something that changed everything. Mitushi was sitting on the floor, humming softly to herself. It was a tune Leela recognized—it was the melody her mother used to sing to her when she was a child. A soft, soothing lullaby that had always brought her comfort. Mitushi had never sung before, and Leela was stunned to hear the familiar notes coming from her daughter.

"*Mitushi*," she said gently, kneeling down beside her. "*That's a beautiful song. Can you sing it for me?*"

Mitushi looked up, her eyes wide with uncertainty. But then, slowly, she began to hum again, the melody flowing from her lips like a delicate thread weaving through the air. Leela listened, tears welling in her eyes. This was the first time Mitushi had communicated something beyond words, something from her heart.

From that day on, music became a lifeline for Mitushi. Her parents filled their home with melodies, playing soft music in the background, singing songs together in the evening, and using rhythms and tunes to help Mitushi navigate her daily routines. It was through music that Mitushi found a way to express herself, to communicate the emotions she couldn't put into words.

The other children still didn't understand her, and Mitushi remained shy and reserved. But slowly, as she became more comfortable with herself, she started to hum in class too. At first, the other kids just watched, confused by this new behaviour. But soon, they began to recognize the tunes she hummed, and some of them even started humming along with her. It was a small connection, but it was the first time Mitushi had felt like part of something, rather than just an observer.

Her teachers noticed the change as well. They began incorporating more music into their lessons, using songs to teach and to create a calming atmosphere in the classroom. They encouraged the other children to join in, creating a bridge between Mitushi and her peers.

Mitushi's journey was far from over. She still struggled with the unpredictability of the world around her, and her need for routine remained strong. But now, she had something to hold onto—a way to communicate that was uniquely hers, a way to connect with others in a way that felt safe and natural.

And as she hummed her tunes, her world began to feel a little less overwhelming, and a little more in tune with the rhythm of life.

***

This story highlights the challenges faced by a young girl with ASD, focusing on her struggles with communication, sensory overload, and social interactions. It also shows the power of finding alternative forms of expression and connection, in this case through music, and the importance of patience and understanding from those around her.

***

A Shadow in the Sun

Rohan sat in the corner of the small living room, his eyes fixed on the television, though he wasn't really watching. His parents were in the next room with his sister, Ananya, who was busy stacking colourful blocks, a task that seemed to occupy hours of her day. His grandparents, who lived with them, were sitting close by, observing Ananya with soft smiles, occasionally clapping whenever she successfully balanced one block on top of another.

Rohan remembered a time when he was the one who received all that attention. His grandparents used to tell him stories about Superheroes, about the Arabian Knights and the festivals they celebrated. His parents used to take him to the park every weekend, teaching him how to fly a kite or play cricket. Life was full of laughter and warmth. But everything changed when Ananya was born.

She was diagnosed with Autism when she was just a toddler. The word itself had meant nothing to Rohan at first, but it quickly became the center of his world. He watched as his parents poured all their energy and time into caring for her, learning everything they could about her condition. They enrolled her in a special school, took her to therapy sessions, and attended countless meetings with the doctors. Rohan, meanwhile, became a quiet presence in the house, almost an afterthought. It seems as though it was assumed that he would comprehend.

His parents would still talk to him, ask him about school or his cricket practice, but there was always a sense of urgency, a need to return to Ananya as quickly as possible. His grandparents, who had once been his refuge, were now equally absorbed in Ananya's world, finding joy in her small achievements.

It wasn't long before Rohan started to resent his sister. He knew it was wrong—she didn't choose to be this way—but it was hard not to feel angry. Whenever she cried, everyone would come running, and Rohan would be left to deal with his own problems on his own. If she hurt herself, the entire house would go into a frenzy, but when Rohan scraped his knee at school, his mother barely glanced up from the dinner she was making.

And then there was the constant attention she received. Everyone in the family, from his parents to his grandparents, seemed to be caught up in a never-ending conversation about Ananya—her progress, her needs, her future. Rohan felt like he had faded into the background, a shadow in his own home.

One evening, Rohan sat on the balcony, trying to focus on his homework, but his thoughts kept drifting. Inside the house, he could hear his parents talking in low voices, discussing Ananya's latest therapy session. His grandparents were with Ananya, helping her with a new puzzle.

Rohan clenched his fists. He knew he should be understanding, but it was hard. Every time Ananya reached out to him, wanting to hold his hand or sit beside him, he would jerk away. The sight of her only reminded him of everything he had lost—the attention, the love, the feeling of being seen.

His breaking point came one weekend when his parents planned a family outing. Rohan had been excited, thinking they would go to the Amusement Park, just like old times. But when they told him they were going to a sensory park designed for children like Ananya, he couldn't hide his disappointment.

"Can't we go somewhere normal for once?" he blurted out, his frustration spilling over. His mother looked taken aback. *"Rohan, this is important for Ananya." "And what about me?"* Rohan snapped. *"Don't I matter anymore? It's always about her! She's the only one anyone cares about in this house!"* His father's expression hardened. *"Rohan, that's enough."*

"No, it's not enough!" Rohan shouted, tears welling up in his eyes. *"I'm tired of being invisible! I'm tired of*

everyone caring more about her than me! I hate this! I hate her!"

The words hung in the air, heavy and cruel. His mother's face crumpled, and his father's stern expression softened into something that looked like sorrow. Rohan's grandmother, who had been standing nearby, looked at him with a mixture of shock and sadness.

Without another word, Rohan turned and ran out of the house. He didn't know where he was going; he just needed to get away.

Rohan found himself at the old playground near his house, a place where he used to come with his father to play cricket. He sat on one of the swings, kicking the dirt beneath his feet, feeling a mixture of anger and guilt. He knew what he said had hurt his parents, but he couldn't help the way he felt.

After what felt like hours, he heard footsteps approaching. He looked up to see his grandfather walking towards him, his face lined with concern. Without saying anything, his grandfather sat down on the swing next to Rohan, letting the silence linger between them.

After a few moments, his grandfather spoke. *"You know, when your father was a boy, he had a younger brother. Your uncle."* Rohan looked up, surprised. His grandfather had never talked much about his family.

"He was born sickly," his grandfather continued. "We didn't know what was wrong at first, but he was always in and out of the hospital. Your father had to grow up faster than most kids because of that. He had to help us with everything, but he never complained. But I knew, deep down, he felt the way you do now."

Rohan frowned. "What do you mean?"

His grandfather sighed. "Your father felt neglected, just like you do now. We were so focused on your uncle's health that we didn't realize how much your father needed us too. It wasn't until much later that we understood how hard it was for him."

Rohan didn't know what to say. He had never imagined that his father had gone through something similar.

"*It's okay to feel the way you do, Rohan,*" his grandfather said gently. "*But it's important to understand that your parents love you just as much as they love Ananya. They're trying their best, even if it doesn't always feel that way.*"

Rohan looked down, his anger starting to melt into something else—something closer to sadness. "*I just feel like I don't matter anymore.*"

His grandfather reached out and placed a hand on Rohan's shoulder. "*You matter more than you know. And it's okay to talk about how you're feeling. You don't have to carry it all inside.*"

When Rohan and his grandfather returned home, his parents were waiting in the living room, their faces etched with worry. His mother rushed to him, pulling him into a tight hug, her tears dampening his shirt. His father stood nearby, his expression soft but serious.

"*Rohan,*" his father began, "*we're sorry. We didn't realize how much you were struggling. We've been so focused on Ananya that we forgot to make sure you were okay too.*"

His mother nodded, wiping her tears. "*We love you, beta. More than anything. And we're going to do better. We'll make more time for you, I promise.*"

Rohan felt a lump in his throat. *"I'm sorry for what I said. I didn't mean it."*

His father shook his head. *"It's okay. We understand. We just want you to know that you're not alone. We're a family, and we'll get through this together."*

For the first time in a long while, Rohan felt a sense of relief. He knew it wouldn't be easy—there would still be moments of frustration, moments when he felt like he was in the background—but he also knew that his parents saw him now. They understood his pain, and they were willing to work through it together.

Over the next few weeks, things slowly began to change. His parents made more effort to include him in decisions, and they started spending more one-on-one time with him. His grandparents also took turns telling him stories again, just like they used to.

And Rohan, in turn, started to see Ananya differently. He still struggled with his feelings, but he tried to be more patient with her, to understand that she wasn't the reason for his pain. She was his sister, and she needed him just as much as he needed his family.

One day, as they were all sitting in the living room, Ananya toddled over to Rohan, her small hand reaching out to him. For a moment, he hesitated, but then, instead of pulling away, he gently took her hand in his.

Ananya looked up at him with a small, contented smile, and for the first time, Rohan felt a flicker of warmth in his heart.

It wasn't a perfect family, and it wasn't the family Rohan had once known or expected. But it was his family, and that was enough.

***

This story is about the struggle of the family members and the caregivers of an Autistic child. It talks about how their life changes to accommodate a child with special abilities in their normal life. It showcases how they struggle to understand their behavioural pattern.

***

Story 7#

The Storm Inside: A Story of a Child's Silent Struggle

Aarav was only 10 years old, but he carried a burden that felt far heavier than he could bear. He was a bright boy, full of energy and curiosity, but there was a storm inside him—a storm that he couldn't control. He was always on the move, fidgeting, running, talking, and unable to sit still for more than a few minutes. His teachers labelled him "hyperactive," but to Aarav, it was just how he was.

The trouble started when his energy turned into something darker. Aarav's emotions, always intense, began to spiral out of control. When he got frustrated, which happened often, his anger flared up like a wildfire. He didn't mean to hurt anyone, but he did—pushing, shoving, and shouting. The other kids in his class started to avoid him, scared of his sudden outbursts. They whispered about him behind his back, calling him "crazy" and "dangerous."

Aarav noticed. He noticed everything, and it only made him angrier. The more isolated Aarav became, the more his anger grew. He didn't understand why the other kids didn't want to play with him. He didn't understand why his teachers were always upset with him, even when he tried his best. Every day felt like a new battle—against his classmates, against his teachers, against himself.

Aarav's teachers, overwhelmed and frustrated, began to see him as a problem rather than a student. *"Aarav, why can't you just sit still and pay attention?"* they would ask, exasperated. *"Why do you have to cause so much trouble?"* Aarav didn't have an answer. He wished he could explain that he wasn't trying to cause trouble that he didn't want to be the way he was. But the words never came out right. Instead, he lashed out, his anger taking control before he could stop it.

His mother was called to the school almost every week. The complaints piled up—Aarav had gotten into another fight, Aarav had disrupted the class again, Aarav had yelled at a teacher. Each time, his mother would try to defend him, but she was growing weary. She loved her son dearly, but she didn't know how to help him. At home, she would gently try to talk to him, to understand what was going on inside his head, but Aarav would just shut down, retreating into silence.

His father, on the other hand, was less patient. He was angry—angry at Aarav, angry at the school, angry at the situation. "*Why can't you just behave?*" he would yell, his voice echoing through the house. "*Why do you have to make everything so difficult?*" Aarav didn't know. He wished he could be different, that he could make his father proud, but the anger inside him wouldn't let go.

The turning point came one day during recess. Aarav was playing by himself, as usual, when a group of boys from his class approached him. They started teasing him, calling him names, taunting him about his outbursts. Aarav tried to walk away, but the anger inside him exploded.

He tackled the biggest boy to the ground, his fists flying. He didn't feel the punches he threw, didn't hear the shouts of the other kids. All he felt was the red-hot rage that consumed him, blocking out everything else.

By the time a teacher pulled him off, the damage was done. The other boy was crying, his face bruised and bloody. Aarav was hauled to the principal's office, his heart pounding, his hands trembling with leftover adrenaline.

This time, the call to his mother wasn't just about another fight. It was about suspending Aarav, about the possibility of expulsion. The principal explained that they couldn't have a student who was a danger to others, that Aarav needed help they couldn't provide.

When Aarav's mother arrived, she was pale and shaking. She held Aarav close, but he could feel her fear, her uncertainty. His father didn't come this time. He was too angry, too disappointed.

That night, Aarav lay in his bed, staring at the ceiling, feeling more alone than ever. The storm inside him raged, but there was no one to talk to, no one who understood. He thought about the things the other kids said, the way his teachers looked at him, the anger in his father's eyes. It all built up until it felt like a crushing weight on his chest, too heavy to bear.

He wondered if things would be better if he wasn't around. If maybe, just maybe, the storm would go away if he did. The next morning, Aarav didn't want to get out of bed. He didn't want to face another day of anger, isolation, and disappointment. But his mother insisted, her voice tired but firm. *"You have to go, Aarav,"* she said. *"We'll figure this out."*

Aarav dragged himself to school, his feet heavy, and his heart heavier. He couldn't shake the feeling that things were never going to get better, that he was always going to be the problem child, the one no one wanted around. During class, Aarav sat quietly, his mind a whirl of dark thoughts. He didn't hear the teacher's instructions, didn't notice the other kids around him. All he could think about was how to make the pain stop.

When the bell rang for lunch, Aarav didn't go to the cafeteria. Instead, he wandered the empty hallways, lost in his own head. He found himself in a deserted stairwell, the sounds of the school muffled and distant. He sat down on the steps, hugging his knees to his chest, and let the tears he had been holding back for so long finally fall.

He didn't know how long he sat there, crying quietly to himself, but eventually, he heard footsteps. He quickly wiped his face, trying to hide his tears, but it was too late. *"Aarav?"* a soft voice said. He looked up to see Ms. Sen, the school's guidance counsellor. She had always seemed kind, but Aarav had never really talked to her before. Now, he felt a lump in his throat as she sat down beside him. *"What's going on, Aarav?"* she asked gently. Aarav didn't answer. He didn't know what to say. But Ms. Sen didn't push him. She just sat there, waiting, her presence calm and reassuring.

After a long silence, Aarav finally spoke, his voice barely above a whisper. *"I don't want to be like this anymore."* Ms Sen looked at him, her eyes filled with understanding. *"Like what, Aarav?"* *"Angry. Out of control. I don't want to hurt people, but I can't stop it. I don't know what to do."* Ms Sen nodded slowly. *"I know it feels like that right now, like you're trapped in your own emotions. But there are ways to help, ways to manage the anger and the feelings that come with it. You're not alone in this, Aarav."* Aarav felt a flicker of hope, a tiny spark in the darkness. *"But what if it doesn't work? What if I'm always like this?"*

Ms Sen gave him a small, reassuring smile. *"It's not going to be easy, and it's going to take time. But with the right support, you can learn how to manage your feelings. You can learn to control the storm inside you."* That day marked the beginning of a new journey for Aarav. With the support of Ms Sen, his parents, and a therapist who specialized in helping children with anger issues, Aarav began to learn how to understand and manage his emotions.

It wasn't easy. There were setbacks, days when the anger felt too strong to control. But slowly, with patience and practice, Aarav started to find other ways to express his feelings. He learned techniques to calm himself down when he felt the storm brewing inside, and he began to understand the triggers that set off his anger.

His parents, too, learned how to support him in healthier ways. His father, realizing the impact of his own anger, made a conscious effort to be more patient, to listen to Aarav rather than react with frustration. His mother continued to be a source of unconditional love, but now she had the tools to help Aarav cope with his emotions more effectively.

At school, Aarav was given a fresh start. Ms Sen worked with his teachers to help them understand Aarav's needs and to create an environment where he could succeed. Slowly, the other kids started to see a different side of Aarav—a boy who was trying his best, who was learning to control the storm.

Months passed, and Aarav's life began to change. The anger that had once consumed him no longer controlled him. He still had moments of frustration, times when the storm inside threatened to break free, but he now had the tools to keep it in check.

He made new friends, kids who accepted him for who he was and didn't judge him for his past. His teachers began to see his potential, praising him for his hard work and determination. The calls from school to his home about bad behaviour stopped, replaced by notes about Aarav's progress and the positive changes they were seeing.

Aarav still had a long road ahead, but he no longer felt alone. He knew that there were people who cared about him, who wanted to help him succeed. And most importantly, he knew that he didn't have to fight the storm by himself.

As Aarav stood at the edge of the playground one day, watching his friends play, he felt something he hadn't felt in a long time—peace. The storm inside him had calmed, and for the first time, he felt like he could breathe.

He smiled to himself, knowing that while the journey had been hard, it was worth it. Aarav had found his way through the darkness, and now, he was ready to embrace the light of a brighter tomorrow.

This story addresses the difficulties faced by kids with behavioural problems. Although they appear to be just another typical child, they are fighting an internal struggle that is too terrible.

Shadows of the Mind

Keshav stared at the ceiling, the fan spinning in slow, monotonous circles above him. The early morning light seeped through the curtains, casting long shadows across his room. It was another day, just like the one before, and the one before that. He felt an overwhelming heaviness in his chest, as if the weight of the world was pressing down on him, making it difficult to even move.

He used to be different. Just a year ago, Keshav was the kind of kid who had dreams, ambitions, and a group of friends he could rely on. He loved playing football, sketching in his notebook, and hanging out at the playground. But something slowly started to change inside him. The vibrant colours of his life had faded into dull shades of grey.

It started slowly, almost imperceptibly. He began losing interest in the things he once loved. His grades, once a source of pride, began to slip. Friends noticed his withdrawal, but he brushed off their concerns with a forced smile and a half-hearted joke. He didn't want to burden anyone with his problems. He didn't want to admit that something was wrong.

The dark thoughts crept in, whispering lies in his ear. You're not good enough. No one really cares about you. You're just a burden. At first, he tried to push them away, but they were persistent, like shadows that grew longer as the days grew shorter. Soon, the thoughts consumed him, filling every waking moment with a sense of despair that he couldn't escape.

His parents noticed the change, of course. His mother, with her gentle voice, asked him *"Keshav, are you okay? You look so pale. Do you want to talk about anything?"* Keshav replied with a forced smile in his face *"No Ma, I am absolutely fine."* His father would suggest going for a run together, trying to connect in the only way he knew how. But Keshav couldn't bring himself to open up. He didn't want them to see how broken he felt inside.

School slowly started becoming difficult. The noise, the people, the constant pressure to perform—it was all too much. He started skipping classes, hiding in the library or finding a quiet corner where he could be alone. But even in solitude, the thoughts followed him, gnawing at his mind.

One day, after a particularly rough night where sleep eluded him and the darkness seemed to close in from all sides, Keshav made a decision. He couldn't keep living like this. He couldn't keep pretending that everything was fine when it wasn't. But he also didn't want to die, not really. He just wanted the pain to stop.

He sat on the edge of his bed, staring at the bottle of pills he had taken from the medicine cabinet. He did not know what medicines these were, neither did he understand the side effect of these medicines. His hands trembled as he held it, the cap already unscrewed. But as he looked at the pills, something inside him hesitated. A small, flickering thought broke through the haze: What if things could get better?

It wasn't a voice of hope, exactly. It was more of a question, a faint glimmer of uncertainty. But it was enough to make him pause. He thought about his little sister, Kiara, who would be devastated if something happened to him. He thought about his parents, who, despite everything, loved him more than anything in the world. And he thought about the life he used to have, before the shadows took over.

Keshav put the bottle down, his hands still shaking. He didn't know what to do next, but he knew he couldn't keep going on like this. He needed help, real help. Not just the superficial "*I'm fine*" he'd been telling everyone, but the truth—the messy, painful truth that he was struggling, that he couldn't handle it on his own.

The next morning, Keshav did something he hadn't done in a long time. He reached out. He texted his mom, asking if they could talk. He didn't know what he was going to say, but he knew he had to say something. When she came into his room, her eyes filled with concern, he finally let the words spill out. He could not arrange his words properly. It was messy and difficult, and there were more tears than he expected, but it was a start.

His parents were scared, but they didn't judge him. They listened. They called a therapist and made an appointment, and for the first time in months, Keshav felt a tiny bit of relief. He wasn't alone in this anymore.

Therapy wasn't easy. It forced him to confront the darkest parts of his mind, to unpack the thoughts and feelings he had buried deep inside. But it also gave him tools to cope, to challenge the negative thoughts that had taken root in his mind.

There were good days and bad days, moments of progress followed by setbacks. But slowly, very slowly, the shadows began to recede. He started to find joy in small things again—a sunny day, a good book, the sound of Kiara's laughter, smell of freshly baked cupcakes by his mother. It wasn't a quick fix, and there were still days when the darkness threatened to pull him under. But now, he had hope. Now, he knew that he didn't have to face it alone.

Keshav's journey wasn't over, but he had taken the first, most important step: he had chosen to fight. And in that fight, he found something he had thought he had lost—himself.

⟞⟝

This story highlights the challenges that children with depression face. On the outside, they may seem like any other typical child, but internally they are battling a profound struggle. It is essential for families to offer unwavering support in every possible way to help them navigate and overcome this difficult situation.

⟞⟝

Echoes of Silence

Aditi sat in the back of the lecture hall, her heart pounding so hard she thought it might burst out of her chest. The professor's voice faded into the background, a muffled noise that barely registered over the roar in her ears. She could feel the familiar wave of panic building, the tightening in her throat, the dizziness that made the room spin around her.

She gripped the edge of her desk, trying to ground herself, to breathe through the overwhelming fear that had no clear source. But it was useless. The panic attacks always came without warning, consuming her in a whirlwind of terror that left her gasping for air.

It started a few months ago, shortly after her second-year college classes began. At first, she thought it was just stress. College was demanding, with its endless assignments, exams, and the pressure to succeed. But as the attacks grew more frequent, Aditi began to realize that it was more than just academic stress. Something deeper was at play, something she couldn't quite put her finger on.

Aditi's childhood had been a fractured one, a series of painful memories tied to her parents' bitter divorce. She was only eight when it happened, but she remembered it vividly—the shouting, the slammed doors, the nights spent crying in her room, wishing for it all to stop. Her parents, once her safe haven, had become distant, consumed by their anger and the complexities of their own lives.

Aditi's parents had both remarried within a few years, each creating new families that seemed to have no place for her. She felt like a ghost, drifting between two homes where she was always the outsider, never truly belonging. Her step-parents were polite, but distant and treated her like a stranger. There was no one she could confide in, no one who truly understood the loneliness that had taken root in her heart.

Aditi had always been the strong one, the one who held it together when everything else was falling apart. She threw herself into her studies, determined to build a future that was different from the past she had known. But the pressure was relentless, and the cracks in her facade began to show.

The first panic attack had struck during an exam. She remembered staring at the paper, her mind blank, when suddenly she couldn't breathe. The room closed in around her, her vision blurred, and she felt like she was going to pass out. Somehow, she had managed to leave the exam hall and stumble into the restroom, where she locked herself in a stall and cried until the attack subsided.

Since then, the attacks had become more frequent, striking at random moments—in class, in the library, even in her own room. She was terrified that someone would notice. She desperately wanted to hide it from everyone, her parents, and her friends. She did not want them to see how weak she really was. She couldn't bear the thought of her parents finding out. They were so busy with their new lives and their new families. She didn't want to be a burden on them.

But as the attacks worsened, Aditi realized she couldn't handle it alone. One day, after a particularly brutal episode that left her trembling on the floor of her hostel room, she made an appointment with the campus psychologist. It was a decision born out of desperation, a last-ditch effort to reclaim some sense of control over her life.

Dr. Patel, the psychologist, was kind and patient. She didn't push Aditi to talk, but gently guided her through the process of understanding what was happening. Over the course of several sessions, Aditi began to open up, sharing the details of her panic attacks, her childhood, and the loneliness that had plagued her for so long.

It was hard, admitting how deeply the past had scarred her. But Dr. Patel helped her see that the panic attacks were her mind's way of processing the trauma she had never truly dealt with. The divorce, the feeling of abandonment, the pressure she placed on herself to be perfect—it all came rushing back, manifesting in ways that Aditi could no longer ignore.

Dr. Patel taught her techniques to manage the attacks when they came—breathing exercises, grounding techniques, and ways to challenge the catastrophic thoughts that fueled her anxiety. It wasn't an immediate cure, but it was a start. For the first time, Aditi felt like she had some control over what was happening to her.

But she still kept it all a secret from her parents. She didn't know how to tell them, didn't know if they would even care. They had their own lives, their own worries, and she had learned long ago not to expect too much from them. So she carried the burden alone, managing her panic attacks in silence, while trying to maintain the appearance of the perfect student and the perfect daughter.

There were still bad days, days when the panic seemed overwhelming, when her studies suffered because she couldn't focus, couldn't think past the fear that gripped her. But there were also good days, when she felt a glimmer of hope, a sense that she was slowly, painfully, moving forward.

Aditi knew she still had a long way to go. She knew that the loneliness wouldn't disappear overnight, that the scars of her past wouldn't simply vanish. But with Dr. Patel's help, she was beginning to understand that she didn't have to be defined by her panic attacks, or by the fractured family that had shaped her childhood.

She was learning to be kind to herself, to forgive herself for not being perfect, for needing help. And maybe, just maybe, one day she would find the courage to tell her parents the truth—not because she needed them to fix her, but because she deserved to be heard.

For now, she took it one day at a time, one breath at a time, holding onto the small victories, the moments of peace that were starting to come more often. It wasn't easy, but Aditi was beginning to believe that she was stronger than she had ever given herself credit for.

And in the quiet moments, when the panic receded and the world seemed a little less frightening, she allowed herself to hope—for healing, for understanding, and for a future where the echoes of her past no longer held her captive.

***

This story reveals how the breakdown of a marriage unknowingly impacts a young child's heart. The fear of losing the secure environment of having both parents together is something that every child dreads. While the couple has the right to be with their chosen partners, as parents, they must navigate the separation with great care for the sake of their child. The fear and pain caused by this experience can be overwhelming for the child to bear later on.

***

Invisible Scars: A Story of Silent Struggles

Gaurav was different. At 8 years old, he was quiet, preferred routine, and found comfort in numbers. Diagnosed with Autism, he often struggled to communicate his feelings and understand social cues. His parents, loving and supportive, had always encouraged him to embrace his uniqueness, but they knew the big school would be a challenge.

When Gaurav started at his new school, he was nervous but hopeful. His previous school which was a play school had been understanding, with teachers who took the time to help him adjust. But this new place felt different—larger, louder, and full of unfamiliar faces. He clung to his mother's hand as she walked him to his classroom, his heart pounding in his chest.

Mrs. Desai, his new teacher, greeted him with a tight smile. She was in her late 50s, with a stern face that rarely showed warmth. *"Gaurav, welcome to our class*," she said in a tone that was more duty than kindness. *"You can sit at the desk in the back."*

Gaurav shuffled to his seat, feeling the eyes of his classmates on him. He didn't like being the center of attention, and he quickly buried his face in his workbook, hoping to disappear.

From the very beginning, Mrs. Desai found Gaurav difficult. He didn't respond to her in the way she expected, often staring off into space when she gave instructions. When he was overwhelmed, he would rock back and forth or hum softly to himself. These behaviours, perfectly normal for Gaurav, seemed to annoy Mrs. Desai.

"Gaurav, stop that humming! It's distracting," she snapped one day as he tried to calm himself during a particularly noisy lesson. Gaurav stopped, his cheeks flushing with embarrassment. The other kids snickered, and Gaurav sank lower into his chair.

Mrs. Desai didn't understand why Gaurav couldn't just *"behave like the other kids."* She saw his need for routine and his struggles with change as defiance rather than a part of his condition. When Gaurav didn't make eye contact, she thought he was being rude. When he took longer to complete his work, she assumed he was lazy.

As the weeks went by, her frustration grew. She began to single him out in class, often making him an example of what *not* to do. *"Why can't you be more like the other students, Gaurav?"* she would say, her voice dripping with impatience.

Gaurav didn't know how to respond. He wanted to do well, but the more Mrs. Desai scolded him, the more anxious he became. He started to dread going to school, where every day felt like a battle he couldn't win.

The bullying wasn't just in the classroom. Mrs. Desai's attitude toward Gaurav began to influence the other students. They saw how the teacher treated him and began to mimic her behaviour. Gaurav became the target of their jokes and whispers.

"Why are you so weird, Gaurav?" a boy sneered one day during recess. *"Why can't you just be normal?"*

Gaurav didn't know how to answer. He didn't think he was weird—he just felt different, and he didn't understand why that was wrong. The more they teased him, the more he retreated into himself, seeking solace in the numbers and patterns that made sense to him.

Mrs. Desai, instead of noticing his distress, seemed to see his withdrawal as further evidence of his inability to fit in. During parent-teacher meetings, she told Gaurav's parents that he wasn't trying hard enough, that he needed to *"snap out of it"* and *"join the real world."*

Gaurav's parents were heartbroken. They knew their son was struggling, but they didn't realize how much until they saw how defeated he had become. He stopped talking about school, and his once bright, curious eyes were now tired and scared.

One day, during math class—a subject Gaurav usually loved—Mrs. Desai asked him to solve a problem on the board. Gaurav stood frozen, the numbers swimming in his head, but he couldn't bring them into focus. The pressure was too much. He began to rock slightly, a coping mechanism that had always helped him before.

"Stop that rocking and answer the question, Gaurav!" Mrs. Desai's voice cut through the classroom, sharp and unforgiving.

Gaurav's hands started to tremble. The room felt too bright, too loud. He couldn't think. The other students were staring, waiting for him to fail. His breathing quickened, and he felt a familiar panic rising in his chest.

"I can't," he whispered, barely audible.

"What do you mean you can't? Of course you can! You just don't want to," Mrs. Desai retorted, her patience long gone.

Tears welled up in Gaurav's eyes. He wanted to disappear, to be anywhere but there. *"I can't,"* he repeated, this time louder, his voice cracking with fear.

Mrs. Desai shook her head, her expression one of disappointment and frustration. *"Go sit down, Gaurav. You're wasting everyone's time."*

Gaurav fled to his seat, burying his face in his hands as silent tears streamed down his cheeks. No one noticed. No one cared.

That evening, Gaurav's mother found him curled up on his bed, clutching a stuffed animal he hadn't touched in years. She sat down beside him, gently stroking his hair. *"What's wrong, sweetheart?"* she asked softly.

Gaurav didn't respond at first, but eventually, he whispered, *"I don't want to go to school anymore, Mom."*

His mother's heart ached at the sound of his words. She had known something was wrong, but she hadn't realized how deeply it was affecting him. *"Why, Gaurav? What's happening at school?"*

Through tears, Gaurav finally opened up about Mrs. Desai, about the other kids, about how he felt like he didn't belong. His mother listened, her anger growing with each word. She couldn't believe that a teacher—someone who was supposed to care for and nurture her child—was treating him this way.

The next day, Gaurav's parents went to the school. They demanded a meeting with the principal and Mrs. Desai. In the meeting, Gaurav's mother spoke with a calm fury, recounting everything Gaurav had told her. They explained to Principal Mam that they as parents of Gaurav were already trying to make things better for him. But these instances in school were making things worse for him. They earnestly requested Principal Mam to understand that if the school is unable to improve his situation, atleast they should not be instrumental in harming him further. The regular instances at school had affected Gaurav deeply and if this continued, then they will be compelled to move him out of this school. Mrs. Desai tried to defend herself, saying that Gaurav needed to learn how to adapt. But thankfully Principal

Mam was having none of it. She completely understood the situation. At her urging, the school quickly took action. Mrs. Desai was put on administrative leave while the situation was investigated, and Gaurav was moved to a different class with a teacher who was trained in special education. His new teacher, Ms Mukherjee, was kind, patient, and understanding. She took the time to learn about Gaurav's needs, adapting her teaching style to help him succeed.

For the first time in months, Gaurav felt safe at school. Ms Mukherjee encouraged his love of numbers, creating lessons that played to his strengths while gently helping him navigate his challenges. She made sure he had a quiet space to retreat to when things became overwhelming. She worked with the other students to help them understand and accept Gaurav's differences.

Slowly, Gaurav began to blossom. His grades improved, and he started to make friends—real friends who liked him for who he was. The invisible scars from his time with Mrs. Desai didn't disappear overnight, but with the support of his family and Ms Mukherjee, he definitely started to heal.

Gaurav learned that it was okay to be different, that he didn't have to change himself to fit in. And most importantly, he learned that there were people who would stand by him, who would fight for him, even when he couldn't fight for himself. In the past, his friends would make him wait in the corridor during lunch breaks, and he would comply with their requests, hoping they would eventually include him in their games or at the least they would talk to him for some time. But now, to his great surprise, his friends began to make him feel valued. They took turns to be with him always. He was never left alone, waiting outside the corridor like earlier times.

Gaurav's story spread through the school, becoming a catalyst for change. The administration implemented new training programs for all the subject teachers, emphasizing the importance of understanding and supporting students with special needs. Mrs. Desai retired quietly, her reputation tarnished by the incident.

Gaurav continued to thrive, growing into a confident young man who no longer feared his differences but embraced them. He knew the road ahead wouldn't always be easy, but with the right people by his side, he was ready to face whatever challenges came his way.

⸺⸺◈◈◈⸺⸺

For any child with special needs, both parents at home and teachers at school play a crucial role in their development. This story emphasizes the importance of subject teachers being trained to work with special children. Without proper understanding, teachers may unintentionally damage these children's innocent minds, making them feel unwanted. These children are aware of their differences and constantly seek reassurance. They are highly sensitive to any form of neglect, whether it comes from a teacher, parent, or close friend.

———◈◈◈———

Through My Child's Eyes

S hreya sat at the edge of her bed, staring at the clock on the wall. It was well past midnight, but sleep eluded her once again. Her thoughts swirled around the events of the day—another meltdown from Aryan, another call from the school, another evening spent trying to soothe her son's frayed nerves. The weight of it all pressed down on her, making it hard to breathe.

It had been two years since she lost her husband, Raghav, in a tragic accident. Overnight, Shreya found herself a widow and a single mother to Aryan, who had just been diagnosed with autism at the age of 18 months. The diagnosis had come as a shock, but Shreya barely had time to process it. Her days were consumed with navigating the complex world of therapies, doctor's appointments, and trying to keep her job as a marketing manager to make ends meet.

Shreya loved her son more than anything, but the challenges of raising him on her own were overwhelming. Aryan's autism manifested in severe ways—he struggled with communication, was hypersensitive to sounds and textures, and often had intense meltdowns when his routine was disrupted. The few words he could utter were often jumbled or repeated, and he rarely made eye contact. Every day was a battle, and Shreya often felt like she was fighting it alone.

The lack of societal support only made things worse. Friends who once visited regularly, began to fade away. She was unsure of how to handle Aryan's behaviour. Family members offered sympathy but little practical help. The neighbourhood kids avoided Aryan, and their parents whispered about him, adding to Shreya's isolation. Financially, things were tight. Raghav's insurance money had covered the basics, but Aryan's therapies were expensive, and the stress of it all was taking a toll on her health.

The school system, too, was a constant source of frustration. Shreya had enrolled Aryan in a mainstream school, hoping that early intervention and being around other children would help him. But the reality was far different. The mainstream school's infrastructure and teaching methods were not designed to accommodate a child like Aryan. The teachers, though had good intentions, were unprepared to handle his needs. They unintentionally caused further harm to the child. Instead of support, Aryan faced confusion, and his self-esteem took a hit. Every time the school called with a new complaint, Shreya's heart broke a little more. She knew Aryan was struggling, but she didn't know how to help him.

One particularly bad day, after picking up Aryan early from school due to another meltdown, Shreya realized something had to change. As she sat with Aryan in his room, watching him rock back and forth for comfort, she made a decision. She couldn't keep putting him through the pain of trying to fit into a world that wasn't built for him. He needed her, truly needed her, and she couldn't be there for him while juggling the demands of her job.

The next day, Shreya handed in her resignation. It was a terrifying step—without her income, the financial strain would be immense. But Shreya had no choice. Aryan needed her more than her job did. She decided to start a small home-based business, something she could manage while caring for Aryan. She had always been good with crafts, so she began making and selling handmade jewellery online. It wasn't much, but it allowed her to be home with Aryan, to give him the time and attention he needed.

But there was still the issue of Aryan's education. Mainstream school had clearly failed him, and special schools were either too far, too expensive, or had long waiting lists. After much thought, Shreya decided to home-school Aryan. It wasn't a decision she made lightly—she knew it would be difficult, especially with Aryan's needs. But she also knew that no one else understood her son like she did, and she was determined to create a learning environment that was safe, supportive, and tailored to his unique needs.

Home-schooling was challenging, but it was also a relief. Gone were the stressful mornings of trying to get Aryan to school, only to have him return home more anxious and withdrawn. Now, they could go at their own pace. Shreya learned to incorporate Aryan's interests into their lessons, using his love for trains and patterns to teach him math and language. They spent time outside in the garden, where Aryan found peace in the rhythm of nature. Slowly, she began to see changes in him. He was still shy, still struggled with communication, but he was happier, more at ease.

Financially, they were barely scraping by. The money from her jewellery business was modest, but it was enough to keep them afloat. Shreya learned to live frugally, cutting out unnecessary expenses and focusing on what mattered most—her son's well-being. There were days when the stress threatened to overwhelm her, when she questioned if she was doing the right thing, if she was enough. But every time she saw Aryan smile, every time he looked at her with those wide, trusting eyes, she knew she couldn't give up.

The future remained uncertain. Shreya worried constantly about what would happen to Aryan as he grew older. Would he ever be able to live independently? What would happen to him if something happened to her? The questions haunted her, but she pushed them aside, focusing on the present, on the small victories they achieved each day.

Shreya found support in unexpected places. Online forums and social media connected her with other parents facing similar challenges. They shared advice, offered encouragement, and reminded her that she wasn't alone. Slowly, she began to build a new community around her, one that understood and accepted Aryan for who he was.

As the years passed, Aryan continued to grow and learn in his own way. He might never fit into the mould that society expected, but that no longer mattered to

Shreya. What mattered was that he was loved, that he was safe, and that he was thriving in his own way. Shreya's journey was far from over, but she had found her strength, her resolve. She had learned to fight for her son, to carve out a space in the world where he could be himself.

And as she watched Aryan play quietly with his trains, humming softly to himself, Shreya knew that she had made the right choice. She had sacrificed much, but she had gained something far more precious—the chance to be there for her son, to guide him, to love him unconditionally. In the end, that was all that mattered.

⟫◈◈◈⟪

This story highlights the challenges faced by a single mother raising a child with autism, focusing on her struggles with societal expectations, financial difficulties, and the need to create a supportive environment for her son. It also emphasizes the importance of resilience, love, and the courage to make difficult decisions for the well-being of one's child.

⟫◈◈◈⟪

Spectrum of Silence

Prachi sat at her usual spot in the corner of the school library, tracing her fingers over the colourful pages of her favourite book. The words on the page danced and twisted, making it hard to focus, but she loved the pictures. They were like a secret language that only she understood.

Prachi had ADHD and Dyslexia. The doctors had told her parents when she was just a little girl, and ever since, she had struggled to keep up in school. The letters and numbers on the chalkboard seemed to mock her, flipping and mixing around until they made no sense at all. She often forgot her assignments or couldn't sit still during class, which made her teachers frustrated. And her classmates? They didn't understand why Prachi was different.

At recess, the other kids played together, laughing and shouting, but Prachi was always on the side-lines. She tried to join in sometimes, but the games were too fast, the rules were too confusing. When she couldn't keep up, they would roll their eyes or whisper behind her back. She could understand their ignorance. It would hurt her, but Prachi pretended not to notice. Most of the time they did not make her a part of their games. She was left alone, and no one noticed her sad eyes.

One sunny afternoon, as the other kids rushed outside to the playground, Prachi stayed behind, staring out the window. She was alone in the class with her colours and drawing book. As she forced herself to be submerged inside the colours of her painting, she felt a gentle tap on her shoulder. She turned to see Ms Divya, the art teacher, standing there with a warm smile.

"*Hi, Prachi,*" Ms Divya said softly. "*I noticed you like to draw during the lunch time. Would you like to help me with a school project?*"

Prachi's eyes widened. No teacher had ever asked her to help with anything before. "*What kind of project, Mam?*" she asked, her voice barely above a whisper.

"*We're creating a mural for the school hallway,*" Ms Divya explained. "*I could really use your creativity. Will you be interested?*"

Prachi hesitated, but something in Ms Divya's smile made her nod. For the first time, someone was asking her to be part of something, not just telling her what she was doing wrong.

Over the next few weeks, Prachi spent her free time in the art room with Ms. Divya. She painted bright, swirling colours and shapes that expressed the world as she saw it—a place where words sometimes got lost, but feelings were loud and clear. As she worked, she felt the frustration and loneliness that had followed her for so long, slowly started to melt away.

One day, a group of her classmates wandered into the art room, curious about the mural. They watched as Prachi carefully added details to her part.

"*That's really cool,*" one of the girls said, surprising Prachi. "*Can we help?*" Prachi looked at Ms Divya, who nodded encouragingly. Taking a deep breath, Prachi handed the girl a paintbrush. "*Sure,*" she said, her voice a little stronger now. "*I could use some help with the sky.*"

As they worked together, the other kids started talking to Prachi, not just about the mural, but about little things—books they liked, movies they wanted to see. For the first time, Prachi felt like she was part of something. The mural wasn't just a project anymore; it was a bridge between her and the world she had always felt separated from.

When the mural was finally finished, the entire school gathered to see it. It was a beautiful, chaotic burst of colours and shapes, just like Prachi's mind. And right in the centre of it all, in big, bold letters, were the words: "*Everyone belongs.*"

As she stood in front of the mural, surrounded by her classmates, Prachi felt a warmth in her chest. She had found her place, not just in the school, but in a world that was beginning to understand her—one brushstroke at a time.

———◦◦◦———

The story touches on the struggles of a girl living with her special abilities, fighting hard to find her place in this big world. She wants her existence to be felt and people understood her true value.

———◦◦◦———